WOMEN IN PRISON

Incarceration Issues:
Punishment, Reform, and Rehabilitation

TITLE LIST

WOMEN IN PRISON

by Joan Esherick

Mason Crest Publishers
Philadelphia

Mason Crest Publishers Inc.
370 Reed Road
Broomall, Pennsylvania 19008
(866) MCP-BOOK (toll free)

13 12 11 10 09 08   10 9 8 7 6 5 4 3 2

Library of Congress Cataloging-in-Publication Data

Esherick, Joan.
  Women in prison / by Joan Esherick.
    p. cm. — (Incarceration issues)
  Includes index.
  ISBN 1-59084-993-0   ISBN 1-59084-984-1 (series)
  ISBN 978-1-59084-993-4   ISBN 978-1-59084-984-2 (series)

  1. Women prisoners. I. Title. II. Series.
  HV8738.E84 2007
  365'.6082—dc22
                            2005029516

Interior design by MK Bassett-Harvey.
Interiors produced by Harding House Publishing Service, Inc.
www.hardinghousepages.com

Cover design by Peter Spires Culotta.

Printed in Malaysia.

Contents

INTRODUCTION

by Larry E. Sullivan, Ph.D.

Prisons will be with us as long as we have social enemies. We will punish them for acts that we consider criminal, and we will confine them in institutions.

Prisons have a long history, one that fits very nicely in the religious context of sin, evil, guilt, and expiation. In fact, the motto of one of the first prison reform organizations was "Sin no more." Placing offenders in prison was, for most of the history of the prison, a ritual for redemption through incarceration; hence the language of punishment takes on a very theological cast. The word "penitentiary" itself comes from the religious concept of penance. When we discuss prisons, we are dealing not only with the law but with very strong emotions and reactions to acts that range from minor or misdemeanor crimes to major felonies like murder and rape.

Prisons also reflect the level of the civilizing process through which a culture travels, and it tells us much about how we treat our fellow human beings. The great nineteenth-century Russian author Fyodor Dostoyevsky, who was a political prisoner, remarked, "The degree of civilization in a society can be measured by observing its prisoners." Similarly, Winston Churchill, the great British prime minister during World War II, said that the "treatment of crime and criminals is one of the most unfailing tests of civilization of any country."

Since the very beginnings of the American Republic, we have attempted to improve and reform the way we imprison criminals. For much of the history of the American prison, we tried to rehabilitate or modify the criminal behavior of offenders through a variety of treatment programs. In the last quarter of the twentieth century, politicians and citizens alike realized that this attempt had failed, and we began passing stricter laws, imprisoning people for longer terms and building more prisons. This movement has taken a great toll on society. Approximately two million people are behind bars today. This movement has led to the

overcrowding of prisons, worse living conditions, fewer educational programs, and severe budgetary problems. There is also a significant social cost, since imprisonment splits families and contributes to a cycle of
crime, violence, drug addiction, and poverty.

All these are reasons why this series on incarceration issues is ex-
tremely important for understanding the history and culture of the
United States. Readers will learn all facets of punishment: its history;
the attempts to rehabilitate offenders; the increasing number of women
and juveniles in prison; the inequality of sentencing among the races;
attempts to find alternatives to incarceration; the high cost, both eco-
nomically and morally, of imprisonment; and other equally important
issues. These books teach us the importance of understanding that the
prison system affects more people in the United States than any institution, other than our schools.

CHAPTER 1.

WOMEN AND CRIME: WHO IS IN PRISON AND WHY?

Like many teens in her situation, Jeanne dropped out of high school when she discovered she was pregnant. This pregnancy would be the first of four, all of which produced children: three by one man, the fourth by another. Neither of the children's fathers helped or supported the young mother, and living with her parents in their tiny low-income housing project apartment proved intolerable. With no other option, the New Jersey woman, now barely out of her teens, went on welfare, signed up for food stamps, and moved out on her own with her four young children. The stress of poverty and single parenting proved too much for Jeanne to bear.

Many factors can lead a woman to commit crimes.

In November 1983, the then-twenty-five-year-old took her children to New Jersey's Cooper River, where she waited for each child to fall asleep—and then dropped all four into the river's swift current. The youngest, a little boy named Jonathan, was only two years old. All four drowned.

Jeanne pleaded guilty to the four murders, explaining that she felt her children were "better off dead." Though diagnosed with ***chronic depression*** and ***borderline personality disorder,*** she received four terms of life imprisonment for her crimes.

Doctors determined that Marlene's mother had a "***schizoid personality*** with ***paranoid*** features," the result of which caused her mother to either ignore or obsess over the young girl. When she was ten years old, Marlene discovered that the mentally ill woman she thought was her "real" mother wasn't her biological mother at all. Marlene's parents, who were well off and stable when Marlene was young, had adopted their daughter

Psychiatric disorders often play a role in women's crime.

An unstable home life can contribute to a teen's criminal activities.

when she was only a day old. Learning of her adoption caused Marlene to long for her other mom, her biological mother—a longing that grew substantially as Marlene's adoptive mother's mental health declined.

By the time she was fourteen years old, Marlene's home life had become volatile and unstable. The teenager's grades dropped; she started shoplifting; she popped pills to handle the stress. These behaviors led to more dangerous ones: black magic rituals, promiscuous sex, tripping on LSD, becoming a "High Priestess of the Satanic Church." By the age of fifteen, Marlene's behavior spiraled out of control; she was arrested for grand larceny (the result of a $6,000 shoplifting spree), drug possession, and weapons possession. When Marlene's adoptive mother threatened to send the troubled teen to a juvenile detention center, Marlene determined then and there to kill her.

Two months later, at Marlene's prompting, Marlene's boyfriend bludgeoned her adoptive mom to death with a hammer and stabbed her with a kitchen knife. When Marlene's father walked in on the grisly act,

NOT ALL INCARCERATION FACILITIES ARE THE SAME

The terms "jail," "prison," and "detention center" do not mean the same thing. Generally here's how they differ:

A jail is a smaller facility run by the county, town, or local government located nearest to the place of the arrest or crime that is designed to hold people for shorter periods of time (usually less than a year).

A prison is a larger, more secure facility run by state, provincial (in Canada), or federal governments and is designed to hold convicted criminals including violent offenders for longer periods of time.

A detention center is where people awaiting trial can be detained; it is also a place where youth, nonviolent offenders, or those with short sentences can serve their time.

her boyfriend shot him four times in the chest. Marlene was present for both murders. After watching her parents die, the then-sixteen-year-old left the scene with her boyfriend, visited friends, ate out, and went to the movies. Early the next morning, the teen murderers drove the two mutilated bodies to an open fire pit in a rural area outside of town, doused the corpses in gasoline, and set them on fire.

A week later, after a coworker became concerned over Marlene's father's absence from work, police discovered the crime. Three days after that, Marlene confessed and took police to the bodies. Prosecutors charged Marlene and her boyfriend with two counts of first-degree murder.

Marlene's boyfriend, who was tried as an adult, was found guilty and sentenced to death in the gas chamber (a sentence that was later changed to life in prison). Marlene, whom the judge said "did encourage, instigate, aide, abet and act as accomplice in the homicides of her parents," was tried as a juvenile, found guilty, and sentenced to confinement at the California Youth Authority from which she would be released on her twenty-first birthday. She served less than four years.

Located in western Africa, Fauziya's home country of Togo supported the ancient practice of female genital mutilation—a coming-of-age ritual in which a girl's sexual arousal center (her clitoris) and labia are surgically removed, and her vagina is sewn nearly shut to protect her chastity until marriage. Fauziya hoped to escape this painful, often life-threatening rite, so she fled to the United States and sought political ***asylum***.

Until immigration officials could decide her fate, the then-seventeen-year-old (who had committed no crimes) was sent to a detention facility—a place where officials could keep her in custody until her immigration hearing with U.S. officials could be arranged. While held in detention, she faced abuse at the hands of her guards, abuse worse than anything she'd endured in her own country. She suffered regular beatings and was forced to wear chains around her ankles and wrists; guards made her stand naked for long periods of time just to humiliate her; to add to her embarrassment, guards refused to provide sanitary napkins when she needed them; and guards made her go through numerous strip searches during which she was forced to undress while guards (male and female) examined her body's every nook and cranny.

A riot in the detention center where she was being held initiated Fauziya's transfer to a county prison in Pennsylvania. Though the guards at this facility treated her well, officials housed her with inmates who had been convicted of crimes, some of which were violent. One inmate walked into Fauziya's cell and issued this ultimatum: "You either give me your apple [fresh fruit is rare in prison] or you sleep with me."

The African teenager had never heard of homosexual behavior between women before, let alone been threatened with it. She was terrified.

TOP CRIMES

Top Five Crimes Committed by Incarcerated Women in Canada
1. Schedule I Offenses (armed robbery, assault, and other violent offenses)
2. Schedule II Offenses (drug offenses)
3. Non-Schedule Offenses (theft, forgery, other nonviolent offenses)
4. Second-Degree Murder
5. First-Degree Murder

Top Five Crimes Committed by Incarcerated Women in the United States
(from the U.S. Bureau of Justice Statistics, 1999)
1. property felonies (burglary, larceny, motor vehicle theft, fraud, forgery, embezzlement)
2. drug felonies (trafficking, possession)
3. other nonviolent felonies not listed above
4. aggravated assault
5. aggravated (violent) robbery

She surrendered her prized fruit to diffuse the tension with the other inmate, who then left her alone.

The U.S. government eventually granted Fauziya's request for asylum and released her. Fauziya Kassindja currently works as an **advocate** for immigrants held in U.S. detention centers and has testified before Congress about her experiences.

Jeanne, Marlene, and Fauziya. All were once ordinary girls in ordinary families that faced an array of troubles as most families do. Their differing backgrounds, circumstances, and behaviors resulted in different life outcomes. During their teens and young adulthood, these women dealt with their circumstances in various ways: two committed crimes and one fled

Drug offenses account for nearly 40 percent of women incarcerated in the United States.

her homeland. All three ended up behind bars. Today, one remains in prison (Jeanne), one left prison after four years and became a heroin addict who prostitutes herself to support her addiction (Marlene), and one became a widely recognized advocate for detained women seeking asylum in the United States (Fauziya).

These three women faced three situations, yet they have this in common: in every case, circumstances drove these women to make choices and take actions that would impact them for the rest of their lives.

These cases, documented in detail in Michael Newton's *Bad Girls Do It: An Encyclopedia of Female Murderers* and a Stop Prisoner Rape 2004 report titled *No Refuge Here: A First Look at Sexual Abuse in Immigration Detention*, illustrate the diversity of women who commit crimes or end up behind bars and the complexity of issues that sends them there. Mental illness, physical abuse, depression, substance abuse, fear, gang or cult affiliations, destructive relationships, poverty, cultural norms or expectations, low self-esteem, overwhelming stress, desperation—any of these and more can be found lurking in the histories of America's incarcerated women.

Because such varying issues send women to prison, many kinds of women from many different backgrounds make up prison populations today. Findings by the U.S. Bureau of Justice Statistics (BJS) confirm the complexity of these populations.

According to the BJS, over one million women—almost 1 percent of the U.S. population—live under correctional supervision (either incarcerated or on supervised release). These women represent nearly 7 percent of all U.S. inmates. Roughly half of all incarcerated women in the United States fall between the ages of twenty-five and thirty-four. Nearly 40 percent committed drug-related offenses to land them behind bars. Even more committed property offenses. Many didn't have jobs at the time of their arrests, and nearly two-thirds did not complete high school.

If nonviolent drug and property offenses provide the most common reasons U.S. women end up in jail, violent offenses come next. Combined, these categories account for more than 80 percent of all female inmates.

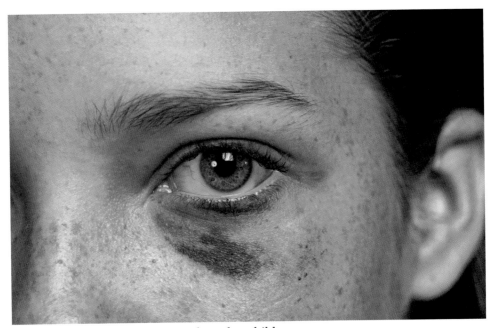

Many incarcerated women were abused as children.

Though the overall numbers are considerably smaller in Canada (Canada's federal prison system held only 345 women in 1999 compared to over 1.2 million women housed in U.S. penitentiaries), Canada's profile of the woman in prison resembles that of the typical U.S. female offender, with the exception of the nature of Canadian crimes. According to the Correctional Service of Canada (CSC), over 50 percent of female inmates in federal facilities in Canada in 1999 were between the ages of twenty and thirty-four. Two-thirds of these (66 percent) were divorced, never married, separated, or widowed. Two out of five female inmates (40 percent) in Canada committed Schedule I offenses (violent offenses like armed robbery or assault), while only one out of four (25 percent) committed Schedule II offenses (drug-related crimes). Though similar in age and marital status, Canadian female inmates were more likely to have been incarcerated because they committed violent crimes.

One characteristic common to both Canadian inmates and women incarcerated in the United States is a history of *victimization*. Of all the circumstances behind North American women ending up in jails, detention centers, or prisons, the most common is physical or sexual abuse.

WOMEN IN PRISON

Consider this case study reported by the CSC. To protect her identity, we will call this offender "Jane."

Jane's stepfather routinely abused her during her childhood and adolescence. She also endured repeated molestations by other family and nonfamily members. What she suffered at the hands of her abusers led Jane to develop what one psychologist referred to as "severe assertive and relationship deficits." In other words, Jane simply didn't have the means or skills necessary to defend herself or stand up for her rights. To deal with her abuse, Jane turned to alcohol.

Jane ended up in a common-law marriage (a long-term living-together arrangement recognized in some jurisdictions as a marriage though no ceremony was performed) to another abuser. With Jane's full knowledge and consent, her common-law husband repeatedly molested Jane's young daughter by another man. This abuse lasted six years and culminated in the girl's rape when she was in her early teens. When Jane's daughter protested, Jane forced the teen to have sexual relations with her stepfather by threatening to hit or punch the girl or take away her privileges if she did not comply. When her daughter refused or complained, Jane beat her. Jane's daughter's scars and bruises testified that she often refused. Finally, the ultimate victim in this tragedy, Jane's daughter, called the police after her stepfather raped her.

Canadian courts convicted Jane of a federal offense (sexual ***exploitation*** of a minor) and sentenced her to three years in prison. In 1994, the government granted Jane full ***parole***, with the stipulations that she have no contact with her daughter, with her former common-law husband, and with any children under sixteen years of age. She also had to agree to counseling.

The CSC reports that Jane is now coming to terms with her past abuse and victimization. Counseling has helped Jane understand why she, an abuse victim, became the co-abuser of her daughter. Jane's alcoholism is being treated and is currently under control, and her once-estranged daughter wants to rebuild their damaged relationship.

In this case, Jane's abusive past damaged her emotionally and led her to become involved in unhealthy relationships, substance abuse, and criminal activity, all of which put her behind bars. She is not alone.

A 1999 CSC needs analysis report on Canada's women offenders cites that 70 percent of Canada's incarcerated women suffered from emotional and past trauma issues. Seventy-five percent abused drugs or alcohol. Seventy percent of those with substance abuse issues also developed psychiatric problems. The study concluded that over half of Canada's female prisoners were prone to self-injury or were at risk for suicide; nearly three-quarters lacked the coping and problem-solving skills they needed to live in the real world.

Private research affirms these CSC findings. The Canadian Association of Elizabeth Fry Societies (CAEFS), a private organization dedicated to helping women involved in the Canadian criminal justice system, estimates that nearly 82 percent of Canada's incarcerated women have survived rape, incest, or physical assault, and that 80 percent ended up in jail for poverty-related crimes. These women committed crimes to survive.

Women prisoners in the United States don't fare any better. According to the U.S. Coalition for Juvenile Justice, up to 73 percent of girls in the juvenile court system in the United States have been physically or sexually abused. Though girls make up only 27 percent of the juvenile court population, they account for nearly 60 percent of juvenile arrests for running away. Dr. H. C. Davis, the supervisor of education at Eddie Warrior Correctional Center in Taft, Oklahoma, describes a "typical" female offender as someone whose history includes substance abuse, low self-esteem, and sexual abuse. Jane, whose offenses were described above, fits this profile almost perfectly: she had been physically and sexually abused before the time of her offenses, she knew her abusers, she developed an addiction to alcohol, and she had a poor self-image.

Most female offenders in the United States fit Dr. Davis's profile, too. A 2004 BJS special report titled *Profile of Jail Inmates, 2002* cites the following statistics:

- Over 55 percent of female jail inmates incarcerated in 2002 used alcohol regularly at the time of their offenses.
- Nearly 35 percent of female jail inmates abused drugs at the time of their offenses.
- Over half of all jail inmates grew up in single-parent homes.

WOMEN IN PRISON

FAST FACTS: WOMEN INMATES IN THE UNITED STATES AND CANADA

- Women make up 12 percent of all inmates in U.S. jails.
- Women make up 9 percent of provincial custody admissions in Canada.
- Women account for nearly 7 percent of all inmates in U.S. federal prisons.
- Women comprise 5 percent of Canadian federal custody admissions.
- Women make up 14 percent of all violent offenders in the United States.
- Women account for over 55 percent of all incarcerated violent offenders in Canada.

- Over 55 percent of female jail inmates had been physically or sexually abused.
- Of these, 92 percent knew their abusers.

Physical, sexual, and substance abuse are not the only issues contributing to a woman's likelihood of ending up in prison. Education, or more accurately the lack of education, plays a role, too.

A 2003 BJS report titled *Education and Correctional Populations* found that two out of every five female inmates (over 40 percent) in U.S. state prisons had not completed a high school education or obtained a GED certificate. A study done six years earlier found that 14 percent of female state prison inmates had completed only eighth grade (or less). On the other end of the education spectrum, only 3 percent had graduated from college. Fewer still held any graduate degrees.

A women's jail facility

Whatever the reasons behind a woman's criminal behavior, the present reality is that hundreds of thousands of women in the United States and Canada live behind bars. More women reside in prisons today than at any other time in history. Today's unprecedented number of incarcerated women creates a number of new issues: where to put convicted women when women's prisons are full; how to handle pregnant offenders; what to do with the many children incarcerated mothers leave behind; how to handle women whose crimes resulted from coercion, assault, or sexual abuse; how to handle women whose crimes resulted from mental health issues or substance abuse; what to do with the rising number of women who commit violent crimes. Most of these issues become painfully obvious in the daily reality of prison life.

CHAPTER 2

WOMEN'S PRISONS: WHAT'S IT LIKE TO LIVE BEHIND BARS?

Imagine waking every morning to your overhead light flashing on and off and the ceiling-mounted speaker blaring, "It's time to wake up," over and over again. Now imagine this happens every day at 6:30 A.M., even on weekends. Once you hear your wake-up call, you have just thirty minutes to brush your teeth, wash your face, comb your hair, get dressed, make your bed, and clean your tiny, bunk-filled room—a room you share with seven others. Inspection and head count occur at 7:00 A.M., and you have to be ready. After inspection, you're sent as a group to the cafeteria, where you grab a quick breakfast

served on a plastic tray, and then head off to class or work or to your program of the day. You can't be late or skip your appointed task; it's simply not an option.

You arrive at work by 7:45 A.M. If you're lucky, you might get to go back to your room at lunchtime, but most girls in your situation don't; they often work or attend class until 3:00 or 4:00 P.M.

When you finish your workday, you return to the building that houses your room, but only a handful of after-work options await you: you can watch TV in the dayroom with other girls; you can go back to your room (which, remember, you share with seven others) and read or write a letter; or you can go out into the yard, a fenced-in outdoor recreation area, often occupied by gangs or your local drug dealers. Whatever you choose to do, you don't have much time. You know you have to report to your room before dinner for another head count.

After guards count everyone, you are dismissed to the cafeteria again for a timed dinner. After rushing through your meal, you return to your unit, where you face the same limited options you faced earlier in the day: read in your room, socialize or watch TV in the dayroom, or walk outside in the yard.

Dorm rules require everyone to return to their rooms by 9:30 P.M. A "lights out" announcement follows on the public address system at 10:00 P.M. You try to fall asleep, but the sound of talking, yelling, and crying rings in your ears.

The next morning, you begin again—same routine, different day.

Welcome to a typical day in a women's incarceration facility. The scenario you've just imagined is an everyday reality for hundreds of thousands of incarcerated women in North America. But this schedule provides only a partial picture of what it's like to live in prison.

In addition to following the structure of this type of schedule, imagine that you also live with others telling you when and how often you may shower, when and if you may use the telephone, when and if you can have visitors, what you can and cannot keep in your room, when you are allowed to leave your room, when and where you can buy toilet paper and tampons, how many clothes you can own, and what kind of clothes and shoes you can wear.

WOMEN IN PRISON

Topics Covered in a Typical Prisoner Handbook

admission	medical services and fees
canteen (prison store)	mental health services
classification	money
conduct, rules of prohibited conduct	personal hygiene
court notices	personal property
dayroom	programs
dental services	recreation
disciplinary procedures	release
emergency procedures	religion
grievance procedures	security regulations
inmate behavior/conduct	sick call and illness
law library	special visitation
library	subsistence and meal fees
living quarters	telephones
mail	visitation

Then imagine that you are given no input into who your roommates will be. They might include drug addicts, prostitutes, shoplifters, or child abusers; they might be people your age or people decades older than you; your roommates might include twenty-year-olds who never made it past primary school or fifty-year-old corporate executives with college degrees; they might be fault-finders or peacemakers, gossips or confidants, racists or humanitarians, heterosexuals or lesbians. Your roommates may wash regularly or rarely bathe. They may wear deodorant or they may not. It doesn't matter. You don't get to choose. You're stuck with whomever you're assigned.

WOMEN'S PRISONS: WHAT'S IT LIKE TO LIVE BEHIND BARS?

Your housing situation isn't the only aspect of prison life in which you have no voice; you also have little or no say in what job you're assigned. You may end up in kitchen services, food service, cleanup crews, yard maintenance, grounds crews, laundry services, office supply and administration, garment repair (sewing), building maintenance, custodial services (cleaning bathrooms and mopping floors), or any one of many other positions waiting to be filled. Prison officials—not you—decide where and how often you'll work.

With your schedule, housing, and vocation already decided for you, you might think that education would be the one area of prison life over which you have some control. Not so; you have no right to education in prison. In general, you cannot take (and will not be allowed to take) courses until you've proven through good behavior that you deserve the privilege of attending classes or learning special skills. Work is mandatory for all inmates; education must be earned. The only control you have is whether or not you exhibit the kind of behavior that will earn you a place in an educational or training program.

As if all of this weren't stressful enough, imagine being isolated from your family, loved ones, friends, your home and neighborhood, and all that you hold dear as you transition from civilian life into the prison system. At a time when you need the support of loved ones the most, you have least access to them.

For many women facing jail or prison time, the most difficult time for them is their transition into the prison system. Entering prison can frighten even the most hardened first-time offender. To ease the transition, most prison systems take a prisoner through several stages of entry.

First, upon conviction and sentencing, the prisoner is kept in a local holding cell or jail until her transport can be arranged from the place of her sentencing to the place of her confinement. Next, she is taken to a van or bus that transports her from the local facility to the place where she'll serve her time. The sentencing judge and the appropriate state, provincial, or federal correctional authority often determine a prisoner's facility assignment—but when the prisoner arrives at that facility, officials there must determine where in that specific facility the prisoner belongs. When

WOMEN IN PRISON

28

Adjusting to life in prison is difficult for women who have been convicted of crimes.

WOMEN IN PRISON

A medium-security prison facility

BASIC TYPES OF PRISONS

Minimum security: for low-risk inmates and first-time offenders convicted of non-violent crimes. These facilities often resemble college campuses, provide housing in open rooms or dormitories, and offer the greatest freedom of movement for inmates.

Medium security: for violent and nonviolent offenders; often a catchall for leftovers from minimum- and maximum-security prisons. These facilities use barred cells that house more than one inmate, restrict inmate movement, and offer closer observation and more security measures.

Maximum security: for high-risk and violent criminals. These facilities house inmates in solitary cells, severely restrict inmate movement (often keeping them in their cells twenty-three hours per day), and provide few amenities. They use high-level security measures: 24/7 video camera monitoring, solid-walled cells, razor wire fences, and other features often associated with images of prisons.

Super Max or Maxi-Maxi: for the most dangerous criminals. Called "control units," these prisons deny inmates all contact with other prisoners, require inmates to wear leg irons and handcuffs whenever they leave their cells, allow inmates to use the outdoor exercise yard only once a week and always alone, and keep inmates in solitary confinement in six-foot by eight-foot cells most of the time.

Once a woman is convicted, the court decides the type of facility where she will be sent.

officials observe inmates on arrival during their initial transitional phase, they determine how great a risk each inmate poses to other inmates (how violent she is; what kind of record she has; what crime she committed; how stable her mental health is; what her behavior suggests about her, etc.). All of these factors contribute toward the decision officials make regarding where the prisoner will be assigned.

When she first arrives at the facility, however, she doesn't immediately enter the general prison population. "Fresh fish," the name existing prisoners give new arrivals, must go through receiving first.

Receiving is a confusing, exhausting, humiliating, and intimidating place for women who have never been to prison. When prisoners first arrive at their incarceration facilities, though specific **protocols** vary from

Prison life is physically and emotionally taxing.

Whatever her crime, a female inmate must prepare herself for the harsh reality of prison life.

institution to institution, they can expect to go through the following in assembly-line fashion:

    to be handcuffed or shackled for transport,
    to completely undress,
    to give up their civilian clothes,
    to go through a strip search (a nude examination with cavity search),
    to shower,
    to be deloused,
    to receive prison-issue clothes (often previously worn and ill-fitting),
    to be called "fish,"
    to be catcalled by other inmates, and
    to be given a brief orientation about rules and procedures.

After completing the reception process, new inmates find out where they will stay for the first few weeks of their confinement—an observation period lasting anywhere from two weeks to several months during which prison officials evaluate an inmate's suitability to prison life, her level of needed security, and other special issues that might impact her long-term housing options and classification.

Inmates in observation typically share a two-person cell with only one other roommate in the observation wing, a luxury that affords greater privacy than they'll experience later on, but that also provides fewer privileges and freedoms than those experienced by the general prison population. As newcomers, women in observation aren't allowed to receive packages, can't sign up for jobs or programs, can't purchase many items from the prison store, and are not as free to move about the facility as others who are already classified.

While the time prisoners spend in observation allows prison officials to perform medical, psychological, behavioral, and educational evaluations on new arrivals, it also allows the incoming women time to adjust to their new surroundings and to get used to the way things operate behind bars. It's a needed adjustment period for inmates and officials alike.

The newly arrived inmates also participate in an admissions and orientation (AO) program during this phase of their incarceration, often

In a maximum-security facility, security cameras monitor all prison activities around the clock.

within the first four weeks of their arrivals. During this program, they receive a prison handbook and lectures outlining prison rules, prisoner rights and responsibilities, and an introduction to daily life at their facility.

Once prisoners complete their AO program and prison officials complete the assessments needed to determine what part of the facility best suits a new arrival, officials classify the new inmate and assign her to a more permanent home in the most appropriate part of the facility. With her new understanding and upgraded status come further adjustments and stress, but also greater freedom.

Some housing facilities offer greater freedoms than others. In both the United States and Canada, prisons and jails are classified by level of security measures taken and are divided into sections called tiers or units designed to hold different types of prisoners within that level of security.

Most women in both the United States and Canada end up in facilities of varying security classifications designed for women only. Canada boasts seven federal prisons for women, five built since 1995. The United States offers nearly a hundred facilities designed exclusively for women. Yet this number is insufficient to house all female inmates in the United States. Because of the shortage of women's prisons, nearly one-fifth of U.S. female prisoners end up in coed facilities, prisons that hold both men and women but that house them in separate units. Officials severely restrict the movements of male and female inmates in these institutions, so much so that contact between men and women rarely occurs.

Regardless of where a woman serves her time, one thing all inmates have in common is this: they lose their right to individual freedom and decision making. This, according to many inmates, is the most difficult aspect of prison life. Inmates do not control decisions about their activities, their lifestyles, and virtually all aspects of prison life. Loss of these freedoms is the cost they pay for committing crimes.

Though prisoners must pay for their crimes, North American governments disallow abuse or neglect of inmates in local, state, provincial, or federal custody. The governments who punish inmates must also take care of them. Food, clothing, shelter, protection from abuse, medical treatment, dental care—these and other provisions allow prisoners to maintain their health and well-being while doing their time.

No prison system, however, is perfect. And women in North American prisons often fall through the gaps. Incarcerated women in the United States and Canada still face special issues.

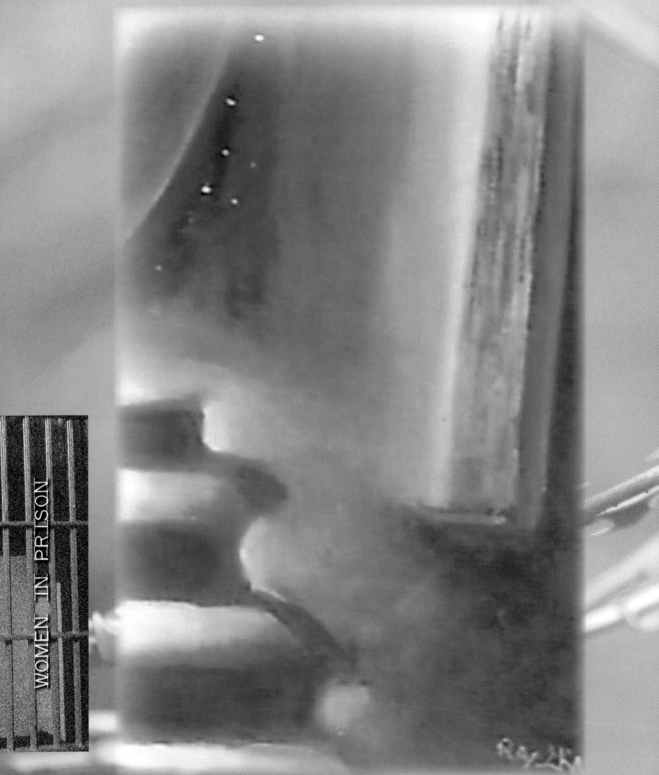

CHAPTER 3

MENTAL ILLNESS, HEALTH CARE, AND OTHER SPECIAL ISSUES FOR INCARCERATED WOMEN

Patty assumes she picked up HIV from dirty needles she used while shooting heroin into her veins before she started serving her time. Once incarcerated, she made history at her prison by being the first woman to stand in front of a Narcotics Anonymous meeting (a gathering of over 150 inmates) and announce that she was HIV positive. No one had ever publicly addressed the issue of AIDS in her prison before.

Patty describes her experience in *The Farm: Life Inside a Women's Prison* by Andi Rierdon:

> I've been in and out of [prison] twenty-nine times—for larceny, prostitution, and possession. In 1989, I found out that I have the virus. For a while I was afraid to talk about it and still practiced risky behavior. . . . Now that I'm at [a different facility] I'm not ashamed that I have this. You don't have to keep an image here. But you do have to deal with what you were running from. . . . In here, there's more compassion and understanding even though we have our bad days.
>
> I max out in fifteen months and I'm scared. It's the first time I'm going to have to live legally without hustling.
>
> But for the time being, I try to learn as much as I can about this disease. I try to keep my mind clear. I'm not afraid of dying from AIDS and I know I probably will because of all the damage I've done to myself. But I try to put all my fears and anxieties to the side because if I don't they're going to stop me from living longer. And that's what I try to tell the other girls. I tell them that they've got to love what life they have left. In some ways, this disease has been a blessing to me.

Unlike Patty, Louise couldn't convince prison officials of her condition. She describes her experience in *Women in Prison: Inside the Concrete Tomb*:

> At the Detention Center, I was pregnant and I knew it, but they wouldn't believe me. They wanted me down on my knees scrubbing the cell block. I was spotting and I told the nurse, but she said, "That's nothing unusual. Everybody spots." But I knew I didn't. I knew I was pregnant and they just didn't want to take me off my hands and knees on the concrete floor. Finally they gave me a rabbit test, and found out I was pregnant—but I was spotting bad.

WOMEN IN PRISON

BARRIERS TO MEDICAL CARE FOR FEMALE INMATES

- irregular and unpredictable sick-call hours
- lengthy waits for medications
- language barriers
- expensive co-pay systems inmates cannot afford
- untrained medical personnel responsible for assessing inmate conditions
- a shortage of substance abuse and mental health programs
- lack of regular preventative health-care opportunities

Before I started bleeding bad, though, they took me down to a hearing in the police paddy wagon with my hands handcuffed behind me. It's just the bare paddy wagon, with no padding. I passed out with my arms behind me and fell off the seat. The cops were pretty decent. They stopped the wagon in the park and let me get out for air.

When we got back from court I didn't feel very good and started bleeding. For ten days I hemorrhaged in the cell—and then I aborted right in the cell. I asked to see the doctor, but he told them to give me an ice bag for my stomach. The girls took care of me. They brought me milk and extra vitamins, but the vitamins didn't do any good then—I had already lost the baby.

When I passed the baby and called for the nurse, she wouldn't even come down until the next day. They wouldn't take me to the hospital until the end, and I was almost dying.

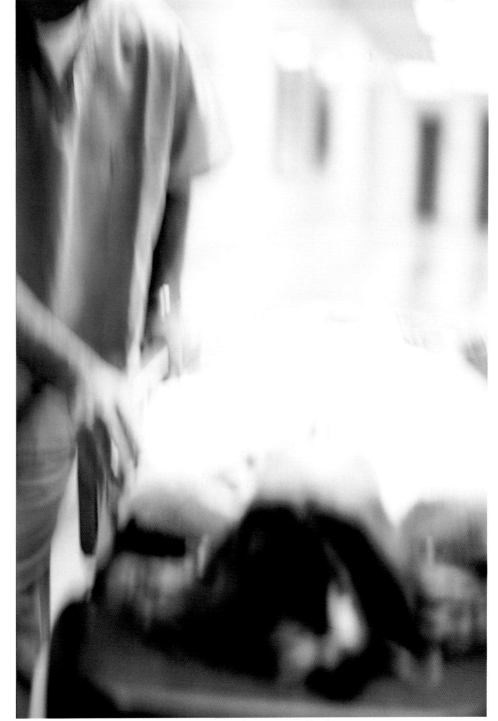

Often, women in prisons do not receive adequate medical care.

OVERLOOKED HEALTH NEEDS OF WOMEN IN PRISON

- prenatal care
- gynecological care
- regular pap smears
- regular mammograms
- annual internal exams by a gynecologist

The prison experiences of Patty and Louise exemplify one issue faced by women in prison today: the need for timely accessible medical care and treatment.

PRISON MEDICAL ISSUES

A three-year-long study completed in 2002 by the U.S. National Commission on Correctional Health Care found that rates of infection for HIV and AIDS were significantly higher among inmate populations than for the general public. In the United States, the prevalence of AIDS was nearly five times greater among prisoners than for those who live outside prison walls. For other diseases the rates are even higher. The rate of infection for hepatitis C, an incurable liver disease, is nine to ten times higher in inmates than in the U.S. population as a whole. Researchers found tuberculosis to occur anywhere from four to seventeen times more frequently among prisoners than the general population.

The BJS found that at the end of 2002, 3 percent of all female jail inmates were HIV positive. A BJS study completed in 1997 found that excluding HIV/AIDS, the most commonly reported medical problems of

Women prisoners face a variety of medical and mental health issues.

inmates in state and federal correctional facilities included heart problems, circulatory problems (other than heart problems), cancer, kidney and liver problems, respiratory disorders (including asthma and emphysema), neurological disorders (including seizures), skeletal issues (joint problems, arthritis, fractures, back/spine issues), and diabetes.

The picture for inmates in Canada isn't much better. A news release issued by the CSC in April 2004 found that federal inmates were more than twice as likely as the general population to smoke or have alcohol and substance abuse issues. Female inmates were more than three times as likely to develop diabetes and asthma, and more than twice as likely to develop cardiovascular conditions.

Canadian inmates in general were more than twice as likely to have hepatitis B, more than ten times as likely to have HIV, and more than twenty times as likely to have hepatitis C as women in the general population.

THE ISSUE OF DRUG ABUSE

Inmates in the United States and Canada get sick just like anyone else, and just like anyone else they need treatment—but medical problems are not the only issue facing women in North American prisons. A BJS report on drug use and treatment in jails found nearly 11 percent of female jail inmates (one in ten) to be actively using drugs during incarceration. Nearly five times that many used drugs at the time of their arrests. In addition to adequate health care, women in prison need help for substance abuse.

MENTAL HEALTH ISSUES

Despite the need for adequate medical care and drug treatment services for women in prison, perhaps the most challenging issue facing prison officials today is how to treat inmates with mental health issues. One study

THE SIX MOST COMMON MENTAL HEALTH ISSUES FOR PRISON INMATES IN THE UNITED STATES

1. anxiety
2. major depression
3. dysthymia (chronic depression)
4. post-traumatic stress disorder
5. bipolar disorder
6. schizophrenia/psychosis

estimates that nearly 25 percent of incarcerated women (one out of every four) in the United States could be categorized as mentally ill. The CSC estimates that Canadian women prisoners are twenty times more likely to develop **schizophrenia** than women not in the prison system, four times more likely to develop depression, and more than twice as likely to develop other mental illnesses. The rate of suicide among Canada's inmates is four times higher than those outside of prison of similar ages.

The international advocacy organization called Human Rights Watch issued these startling statistics in October 2003: one in six prisoners in the United States suffers from mental illnesses including schizophrenia, **bipolar disorder**, and major depression. That means nearly three times as many individuals with mental health issues live in U.S. prisons than reside in U.S. mental health facilities. Many people with mental illness simply cannot get the help they need.

According to one researcher, part of the problem is that women in prison face two realities concerning mental health issues. First, most women with mental health problems who end up in prison are not ad-

Women in prison who have mental health problems are not likely to receive the help they need.

equately diagnosed and treated. Second, those who are often face living with the **stigma** of being labeled "mentally ill." Either they don't get the right help they need or they don't want it.

The complexities of mental health problems and treatment for imprisoned women cannot be addressed adequately in this book. Neither can this book offer a complete look at other health issues and substance abuse challenges women in prison face today. One thing is for certain, though: women in prison need mental and physical health services every bit as much as women on the outside do. And today's correctional services in both Canada and the United States, though they're increasingly aware of the needs and are taking steps toward helping women in their custodies, still have a long way to go.

Many problems remain. Sexual abuse behind bars is yet another issue, a particularly serious and painful one, that confronts imprisoned women everywhere.

MENTAL ILLNESS, HEALTH CARE, AND OTHER SPECIAL ISSUES
FOR INCARCERATED WOMEN

47

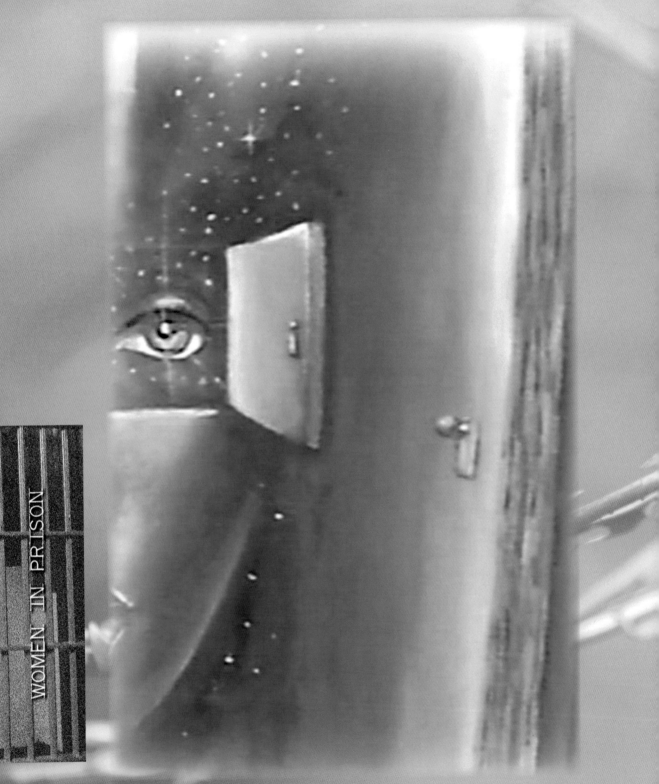

Chapter 4

Safe Behind Bars? Women Guarded by Men

Before her incarceration, Charlene (not her real name) had been a professional concert promoter. Well educated, she made a decent living. Though convicted and sentenced to incarceration for a nonviolent crime, Charlene thought she'd get through her confinement relatively unscathed. She knew that as a nonviolent offender she'd serve the bulk of her sentence in a minimum-security facility with other women inmates and female guards.

She didn't count on being sexually assaulted by the male guards who were responsible for transporting her there.

Her horrifying account, published by the advocacy organization called Stop Prisoner Rape, recounts three days of torture and confinement in a van while being driven from state to state by a private prisoner transport company. Her victimizer, a former Texas Department of Criminal Justice guard who'd been fired for assaulting a male prisoner while on the job, worked for the private company as a transport guard. He'd been assigned to take Charlene from where she was detained in California to another incarceration facility in Colorado. The transport van was scheduled to pick up other detainees along the way.

Charlene's guard, a man we'll call Bill, opted to drive while his partner, a trainee we'll call Sam, slept. Minutes after Sam fell asleep, Bill began making sexual comments to Charlene, who sat alone and shackled in the back of the van. His comments grew more graphic, angry, and bold as the ride continued.

After picking up another female convict in a different part of California, Bill started in on the new woman with the same verbal harassment he had inflicted on Charlene. He refused to allow either woman to take restroom breaks even after hours and hours of riding in the van. He also refused them food and water. Several more hours into their drive, the guard's words took a violent turn.

"I should just take you both out in the desert, rape, and shoot you," Charlene recalls him saying as they crossed the California desert and headed for Las Vegas, where they were to pick up another inmate for transport.

As they approached the state of Arizona, Bill threatened to take the women over the border into Mexico, where he told them he would force them to have sex with him. He boasted that U.S. authorities had no jurisdiction there; he had complete control over the two women and no one could stop him.

The female prisoners, now terrified, exhausted, and completely dehydrated after riding in the hot transport van with no water while cuffed in leg shackles and belly chains, decided they needed to do something. They determined that whatever happened, they would report Bill's behavior.

WOMEN IN PRISON

Sexual misconduct by prison workers puts female prisoners at risk for sexually transmitted diseases, including AIDS.

Women in prison are especially vulnerable to abuse by the guards who are meant to protect them.

Consequences of Sexual Misconduct for Female Victims

- risk of contracting sexually transmitted diseases
- risk of contracting hepatitis
- risk of contracting HIV
- risk of pregnancy
- risk of suicidal behavior
- risk of increased substance abuse
- emotional trauma (depression, shock, post-traumatic stress disorder)
- physical trauma (injuries sustained during the abuse)
- panic attacks
- inability to sleep
- uncontrolled rage
- chronic anxiety
- stress-related physical conditions (ulcers, high blood pressure, etc.)
- shame
- withdrawal
- nightmares and flashbacks

Midway through their ordeal, the prisoner transport company radioed that the van needed to turn around and pick up another federal prisoner, this one male, who was headed for a facility in Oregon. This state-to-state transit route took three and one-half days in all. Bill finally snapped.

At 5:00 A.M. on the third day in the van, Bill uncharacteristically suggested they take a rest stop. Bill and his trainee-assistant Sam escorted the lone male prisoner to the men's restroom, leaving Charlene alone

in the vehicle. The guards had previously delivered the second female to her destination; Charlene was the only female prisoner remaining in the van.

Bill returned from the men's restroom alone; Sam and the male prisoner were nowhere in sight. Bill told Charlene to go to the restroom, something he'd denied her most of the trip in an effort to demonstrate his control over her. Charlene knew something was up when he followed her into the women's empty facility, a place prohibited to men.

There, with no one else in the room, Bill sexually assaulted the helpless inmate, threatening to shoot her if she refused his advances, claiming that he'd say he shot her as she attempted to flee. Charlene had no choice but to comply. She still had to survive the rest of her transport.

After the assault, as luck or grace would have it, the van broke down, and through a series of events, Charlene ended up on a different transport van with a different guard. The traumatized convict arrived at her new correctional facility in shock, severely dehydrated, and bruised from what Bill had done to her earlier that day.

Charlene kept the pact she'd made with the other female convict who'd suffered Bill's tirade during their tortuous van ride; she reported him to the authorities. Attorneys from the American Civil Liberties Union (ACLU) picked up Charlene's case and in April 2002 filed suit against her attacker and the transport company for which he worked. Her case received national attention. Charlene settled with the company out of court for a substantial financial amount, out of which she plans to establish a nonprofit foundation dedicated to stopping victimization of men and women detainees and advocating for those who have been victimized.

Sadly, Charlene's experience with Bill is not unique. According to researchers in the midwestern United States, as many as one in four (27 percent) women inmates surveyed reported having been the victim of coerced sexual misconduct by a guard or prison employee. Despite this fact, as of 2002 only three states in the United States of America—Oregon, Alabama, and Vermont—had no laws on record prohibiting sexual contact between prisoners and those who guarded or worked with them. Women in prison may be protected from abuse by law in most states and provinces, but sexual misconduct still occurs.

WOMEN IN PRISON

Researchers found that as many as one in four female prisoners had been sexually abused by a prison employee in the midwestern United States.

THE REASON FOR SEXUAL MISCONDUCT

Experts say that part of the problem is prison overcrowding. According to the latest U.S. Department of Justice statistics, over two million men and women are now behind bars. The International Centre for Prison Studies states that over 8 percent of these are women. That translates into over 160,000 women incarcerated in the United States. In Canada, where prison overcrowding is less of a problem, the International Centre for Prison Studies estimates the number of incarcerated women to be substantially less: just under 2,000.

U.S. incarceration facilities aren't designed to house this many residents. If you put too many inmates into overcrowded facilities with too few guards, you get increased opportunities for abuse.

Prison guards, employees, and policy makers should know how to prevent sexual misconduct between employees and inmates. They certainly have enough guidelines. Not only do state and federal laws outline and prohibit sexual misconduct, but international laws do, too.

INTERNATIONAL LAW

An international law ratified by the United Nations (UN) in 1992 gave prisoners certain rights. This law applied to American prisoners in the United States and Canada as well as in many other countries around the world. Called the International Covenant on Civil and Political Rights, the law established certain rights for all people, including prisoners, some of which included "the right not to be subjected to torture or cruel, inhuman or degrading treatment or punishment" (Article 7); "the right of any detained person to be treated with humanity and with respect for the inherent dignity of the human person" (Article 10); and "the right to privacy without arbitrary interference" (Article 17). UN interpreters of this

Within the barbed wire fences, many American prison facilities are overcrowded.

law established that this right to privacy also included the mandate that all body searches be conducted only by guards of the same gender as the detainee. Male guards are not supposed to search female inmates.

The United Nations ratified an additional agreement in 1994 that also protects prisoners in the United States and throughout the world. Called the Convention Against Torture (CAT), this treaty established a standard by which countries would handle their confined prisoners. One important protection for women inmates came when CAT identified the rape of an incarcerated woman by a correctional officer entrusted with her care as a form of torture (by international definition). CAT forbids torture in all its forms, and those nations that are part of the treaty, the United States and Canada included, agree to and follow CAT guidelines.

Prison guards are not permitted to spy on inmates or watch as they dress and undress—but those things still happen.

LEGAL RECOURSE

State (United States), provincial (Canada), federal, and international laws protect women detainees in North America. Because of these pro-

SEXUAL MISCONDUCT IS NOT LIMITED TO HAVING SEX

State and federal laws define sexual misconduct as rape or voluntary sexual intercourse between inmates and prison employees, *as well as* any of the following:

- kissing
- touching
- voyeurism
- a guard unexpectedly walking in on an undressed inmate
- a prison official making suggestive remarks about an inmate's body
- offering to trade favors or privileges for sexual contact
- unnecessary strip searches
- unnecessary body searches
- unnecessary cavity searches (looking in a prisoner's rectum or vagina)
- a prison employee showing his body to an inmate
- a prison employee requiring an inmate to show her body to him

tections, women who experience abuse at the hands of their captors do have recourse. Just as Charlene did, whose story opened this chapter, women in America, even imprisoned women, have the right to press charges against the perpetrators of their abuse. These victimized women can do something. And they often find legal assistance and support.

Because of the unspoken rules of the "convict code," inmates silently suffer the abuse of fellow inmates.

SEXUAL ABUSE BETWEEN PRISONERS

Women who suffer at the hands of fellow inmates, either male or female, don't fair as well. Often they suffer silently for fear of **retribution**.

The culture in a women's prison—the way women interact with each other—differs substantially from the culture outside. Inmates expect other inmates to follow not only prison rules but also a set of inmate rules and expectations known as the "convict code." To successfully navigate the prison world, inmates learn to abide by both sets of rules.

Common rules from the convict code for women include statements like these:

Take care of each other.
Take someone under your wing.
Do your own time.
Mind your own business.
Don't touch or steal another's property.
Fight your own battles.
The guards and police are not your friends.
Don't snitch (tell on another inmate).

The last rule listed here is the most widely enforced. If you tell, the inmates maintain, you pay (through beatings, shunning, or other abuse). The code's prohibition against talking to guards about problems with other inmates ("ratting," "snitching," "telling") is what causes many women to stay quiet and put up with mistreatment by others.

Lexi's experience, as described in *In the Mix: Struggle and Survival in a Women's Prison,* illustrates how fear of being labeled a "rat" or "snitch" can keep an inmate from asking for help. The following story, adapted from her original account, describes what happened:

I was stabbed by my roommate. . . . She was my homosexual partner and she started getting involved with heroin . . . so I told her I

SAFE BEHIND BARS?

was moving out. I tried to move out but the regular staff was on vacation. . . . [The replacement] staff asked me if I was having a problem. I knew he could tell. I wanted to tell him that I really was having a problem, but I didn't want to get a rat jacket [a reputation for telling on other inmates].

I told [my roommate] I wanted to move, but she thought I was playing. . . . I didn't want to fight anybody. I was trying to get myself out of that situation. . . . I had hoped to move that night. [The staff] told me I had to wait until [the next day] to move. . . . [My roommate and I] started fighting about 10 P.M.

I went to the room and we were yelling. We were throwing stuff around. I grabbed her and we started fighting. The scissors were in the room, the blade was 8 inches long. They were just there; we had taken them from the . . . laundry—it was not planned. I was beating her and she said, "I am going to stab you."

She stabbed me seven times; she bit me. I blacked out. I didn't realize I was stabbed until I stood up.

Lexi survived her ordeal. But her situation illustrates how fear of being labeled an informant keeps women inmates from getting the help they need. Staff members, even replacement staff in this case, suspected a problem, but Lexi maintained the convict code. She would not tell on her roommate.

Despite horror stories like this one, violence between women inmates isn't as common as you might think. Researchers report that most inmate-on-inmate violence between women involves younger women affiliated with prison gangs or drug trade.

PRISON SUPPORT NETWORKS

For many imprisoned women, fellow inmates become "family": older women assume roles as mothers or grandmothers; women of similar ages become sisters or lovers; most find newcomers to take under their wings. By far, most female inmates just want to feel safe and cared for. One in-

mate put it this way: "Most of the girls are just like us. They all want to go home, get back to their families. Everybody wants to go home to a loved one. . . . You just have to be yourself. The majority of people here respect you." Unlike male prisoners, women build support networks, a sense of family intimacy, that helps get them through the prison experience.

One motivation for the family-like connection many women inmates experience with fellow inmates is loneliness. Another is a longing for security; they want to know someone is covering their backs. For many, however, connections with other inmates fill the voids most inmates experience when they leave their real families behind.

SAFE BEHIND BARS?

CHAPTER 5

Family Affair:
Incarcerated Women and the
Families They Leave Behind

"I'm doing one to three years for fraud," [Dessie] says. "I had food stamps from two counties, and it was my first offense. I offered to give them back or pay for them. [There] was a hundred and sixty dollars' worth, but they wouldn't let me turn them back in or pay for 'em. It was just a small hick town. . . . It was the first time the judge had a chance to send someone to Marysville [Prison], so he sent me. He could have given me probation because I have no past record whatsoever.

"I have seven children and two stepchildren, plus over the years I've had five foster children. They're all with my husband now, but it's really hard for him working and taking care of them, too.

"I regret having had those food stamps so many times. See, I signed up for food stamps in [one county] . . . before we moved to [another county]. After we moved I kept the food stamps from [the first county]. So when they discovered . . . I still had food stamps from [both counties], they issued a warrant. I'd a gladly paid 'em back or done probation.

"This way breaks your home up. It's January now and I haven't seen my kids or husband since November. They tried driving up before Christmas, but the car broke down and now it's still broke down, so they have no way to come up."

INCARCERATED MOTHERS

Dessie's story, which comes from *Women in Prison: Inside the Concrete Tomb* by Kathryn Watterson, illustrates one of the greatest challenges the growing number of incarcerated women presents to society: what to do with their children.

One study estimates that fully one-third of presently incarcerated women lived with and cared for their children at the time of their arrests and imprisonments (the other two-thirds either had grown children, had custody of only some of their children, or were not the primary caregivers). The U.S. BJS estimates the number of women who lived with at least one child at the time of their arrests to be closer to two-thirds of all incarcerated mothers. Nearly 80 percent identified themselves as mothers. Once courts send these women to prison, the fate of their dependent children is out of the inmates' hands.

In Dessie's situation, her husband stepped up. He remained in the picture and assumed responsibility for the children. Statistically, however, few women have this option. In a 1999 study done by the Child Welfare League and the Federal Center for Children of Prisoners, only 28 percent of state-held women and 30 percent of federally held women reported that their children's fathers assumed custody of their depen-

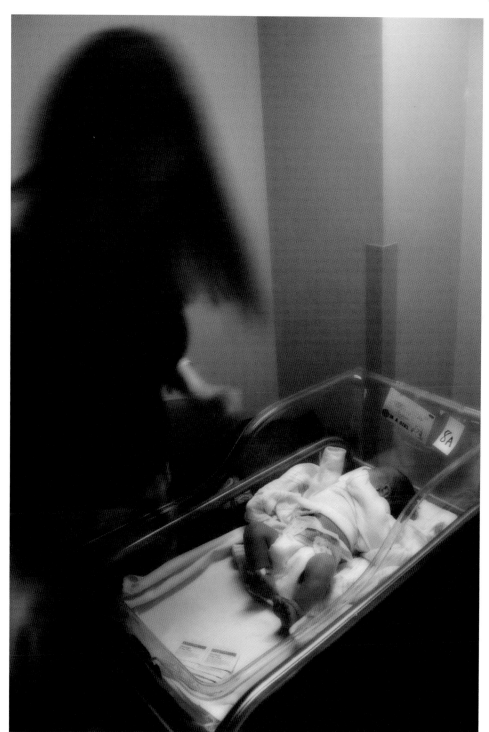

Motherhood complicates incarceration issues.

FAMILY AFFAIR

Children, too, are impacted by their parents' offenses.

dent children during their incarcerations. Nearly 70 percent reported relying on their mothers, sisters, or other relatives to fill the gap while they served their time.

Patty's story, as described in Barbara Owen's *In the Mix: Struggle and Survival in a Women's Prison*, typifies many experiences:

When I had my son, my mom and my aunt took the baby home. On the streets, I was into drugs more than I was into my family. I knew my baby would be better off with my family than with me.

It's been so long since I have seen my kids. I feel like my heart has been ripped out, even though I know I brought myself here. It makes me angry with myself. It still hurts, even if I know my daughter is being well taken care of. I was fighting with my husband on the streets; it was my troubles on the street that brought me here.

Another inmate, Daisy, describing her experience to the same author, illustrates what can happen when other family members assume care for an incarcerated mother's children. Not only does imprisonment separate her physically from her children, but it also can result in damaged relationships:

I have a fourteen-year-old son. I want him to finish school or go in the service, so he can get what he wants out of life. My kids seem to think it is alright that I am in prison. That is all they have ever known about me.

Most mothers are not able to keep their children with them while they're incarcerated.

Saying good-bye may be one of incarceration's hardest blows.

I don't go see him. My sister cannot stand me. My sister took my boys when my mom died. Last time I was arrested, for weapons possession, she wrote me and told me not to come around her house when I was released.

If an inmate's spouse or family will not or cannot care for her dependent children, the courts may step in and place the child(ren) in foster care. Sometimes these arrangements are temporary: the children are placed with a foster family for the duration of their mother's imprisonment and are reunited with their mother on her release. Other times, courts end inmates' rights to parent their children and make the children available for permanent adoption by other families.

Authors Merry Morash and Pamela J. Schram, in their work *The Prison Experience: Special Issues of Women in Prison*, assert that twenty-five states enacted special laws to terminate the parental rights of incarcerated women. They describe these laws as falling into four categories:

1. Laws that take an inmate's children away simply because she committed a crime, regardless of the offense.
2. Laws that take an inmate's children away because of how serious her crime was.

3. Laws that take an inmate's children away because she did not maintain contact with her children while she was in prison or because she cannot provide a stable home environment upon her release.
4. Laws that take an inmate's children away because imprisonment severely damaged the parent–child relationship or the inmate would not have the ability to assume full responsibility for her children on her release from prison or jail.

Despite the hurdles imprisoned women must overcome to maintain contact with their families, many do. Family contact is important to them. According to a 1990 study done by the American Correctional Association, more than 50 percent of women surveyed identified their children as their most important relationship at the time of the survey. Nearly 20 percent identified their mothers as most important. Only 10 percent identified a spouse, boyfriend, or common-law husband as primary.

This importance of family dominates the lives of many female inmates. Many make ongoing contact with their children a priority. Some women write letters or postcards to their children daily; others write every other day. Some call their children from their units' telephones two or three times a week. Still others keep their children's pictures and letters taped to their cells' ceilings and walls.

While letter writing and phone calls make up most regular contacts women have with their children, some women, if they are allowed, enjoy face-to-face visits with their families at their facilities' visitor centers. Prison visitation rules usually limit these visits to no more than twice a week for no longer than twenty minutes at a time, and they often don't allow physical contact: mothers can't hold or hug their children. As of 1994, 75 percent of prisons in the United States did not allow contact between inmates and visitors.

Despite the no-contact rule and short time limits, most inmates relish personal visits. Yet face-to-face visits are the exception rather than the norm. Personal visits can sometimes be difficult to arrange. Consider these criteria: a woman must be sent to a prison or jail close enough for her children to visit; her children's caregivers must be willing and able

If no spouse or family member can take care of an inmate's child, the child may be put into foster care.

FAMILY AFFAIR

In some states, when a mother is put behind bars, she risks losing custody of her children permanently.

to make the trip; her children must want and be able to visit; and the inmate must want and be allowed to see her children (sometimes women lose visiting privileges because of behavioral issues). Sadly, the likelihood of all four criteria being met at the same time is slim. As such, face-to-face contact between inmates and family is the least common method of maintaining contact between an incarcerated woman and her children.

Juana's situation, adapted below from *The Prison Experience: Special Issues of Women in Prison*, illustrates the challenges women face in trying to maintain face-to-face contact.

Juana's children, who were ages seven, nine, and twelve at the time of her arrest, had always been in her care. Arrested on drug-related charges, this stay-at-home mother of three was sentenced to serve two years in prison. After a short stay at a local facility and only two short visits with her children, prison officials transferred Juana to a facility hundreds of miles from her home and from the home of her mother, who had been given temporary custody of the children while Juana served her time. After the transfer, although Juana wrote regularly to her children, the foster-care agency that granted custody of the kids to Juana's mother decided the distance between Juana's facility and where her children lived was too far to maintain contact. Rather than asking the court to move Juana to a facility closer to home, the foster-care agency simply left the young mother out of the decision-making processes for her children. Her mother gained full custody of the three children, and Juana lost all parental rights.

PREGNANCY IN PRISON

As traumatic as these situations are for incarcerated mothers, imagine what it would be like to discover you're pregnant when you get to jail. The U.S. BJS estimates that in 1997, over 6 percent of women inmates with children gave birth to a child while serving their time. That's what happened to the following unidentified inmate whose interview in *In the*

Due to many factors, personal visits are uncommon for women in prison; family members must write letters to keep in touch.

Mix: Struggle and Survival in a Women's Prison describes what it was like to give birth while serving her time:

> [When you go into labor the ambulance comes quickly.] An officer goes with you and stays with you—you are on the [hospital] ward with other women, but they don't put anybody from the [free] world in with you. You are not allowed visitors. You can keep the baby in the room, but you are lucky to have twelve hours with the baby—usually you have between six to eight hours. I still have the feeling of being empty: must be the baby blues. I can remember walking out of his room, turning around and looking at him—knowing I was leaving him. Even though my mom and [the baby's] dad picked him up, I still don't know where he will live. I don't know who will take care of him.

Another woman in the same study described her feelings this way: "It's hard when you are pregnant here. You are so full of life and then you have the life taken away. You are depressed."

Women who give birth in U.S. prisons are generally not allowed to keep their babies, although a few minimum-security institutions are trying new programs to maintain the mother–infant bond. Boston's Neil J. Houston House offered the first community-based program for pregnant offenders in the United States in 1988 and has become a model agency for other programs today. Pregnant inmates soon eligible for parole from Massachusetts' incarceration facilities are eligible to participate in the Houston House's residential treatment program. The house, which can room fifteen mothers and their infants, maintains a twenty-four-hour supervisory staff, an alarm system, and random drug-testing protocols to ensure a secure facility. The program also offers therapies, parent education classes, well-baby clinics, and medical care through a local hospital to help former inmates make the transition from incarceration to community living and healthy motherhood.

Melise's story, as reported in a *Globe* article in December 2001, illustrates the dramatic impact this kind of program can have on the lives of inmates and their children. If it weren't for Houston House, Melise might

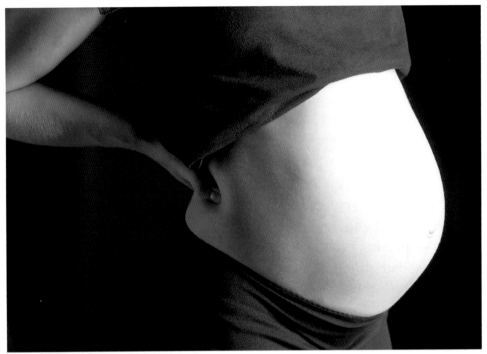

Pregnant inmates have few options.

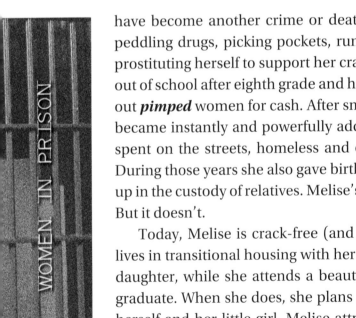

have become another crime or death statistic. She spent twenty years peddling drugs, picking pockets, running scams, and, for a short time, prostituting herself to support her crack cocaine addiction. She dropped out of school after eighth grade and hooked up with a guy she later found out *pimped* women for cash. After smoking crack her very first time, she became instantly and powerfully addicted. The next eighteen years she spent on the streets, homeless and constantly looking for her next fix. During those years she also gave birth to six children, all of whom ended up in the custody of relatives. Melise's story could have had a sad ending. But it doesn't.

Today, Melise is crack-free (and has been for four years now). She lives in transitional housing with her seventh child, a twenty-month-old daughter, while she attends a beauty school from which she will soon graduate. When she does, she plans to work as a hairdresser to support herself and her little girl. Melise attributes the dramatic turnaround in her life to her last imprisonment and her stay at Houston House.

Some women have many difficult issues to overcome before becoming good parents.

Programs like Houston House help women get back on their feet and become better role models for their children.

Melise says that Houston House's main programs and rules—no drugs, no violence, no sexual acts, no bad rapping—helped her stay clean throughout her pregnancy, supported her through her pregnancy and delivery, and helped her get her life back on track. She's become a clean, sober, lovingly attentive mother who is capable of caring for and financially supporting her children.

Since her turnaround, this former crack addict has worked hard to establish closer ties to her first six children, with whom she now communicates weekly. And she is responsibly raising her seventh and youngest child, the little girl she bore while staying at Houston House. As if trying to make up for lost time, she reads five books a day to her young daughter. Her newfound commitment to excellent parenting is remarkable and exemplary. Her growing skills and increased understanding testify to the impact programs like those at Houston House can have on women in prison.

If only all countries around the world afforded female inmates the same opportunities that Houston House and programs like it provide women convicts in the United States and Canada. Sadly, this is not the case.

WOMEN IN PRISON

82

CHAPTER 6

INTERNATIONAL OFFENDERS: IMPRISONED WOMEN AROUND THE WORLD

All she wanted was another baby. But Lin (not her real name), a young mother of two, lived in a nation that restricted the number of children a woman can bear. When Lin became pregnant with her third child, her employers fired her and informed the police of her condition. The police arranged a forced abortion and ensured the young woman would never get pregnant again.

Believing she'd been unjustly treated by the police and unfairly terminated from her job, Lin followed official procedures asking authorities to investigate her firing and the treatment she received when her pregnancy was terminated. Though officials discouraged her from pursuing the matters, she steadfastly refused to drop her search for justice.

Her persistence infuriated officials. In retribution, police detained Lin several times and committed her to a psychiatric hospital where doctors forced her to undergo electric shock treatments. In April 2004, officials, who by then were fed up with Lin's petitions, sentenced the young woman to serve eighteen months in a "re-education through labor camp." Her *crime*? Pursuing **redress** for how police treated her and for what she felt was unjust termination from her job.

Amnesty International, an international human rights **watchdog** group, reports that since her incarceration, Lin has twice suffered torture at the hands of her captors. In the first instance, guards suspended her by her wrists from a ceiling and beat her. In the second, guards secured straps around Lin's wrists and ankles and stretched her four limbs in opposite directions, saying they wouldn't stop until she confessed her wrongdoing. They continued this painful stretching torture for over two full days.

Lin still refuses to admit any wrongdoing and refuses to sign any documents or confessions indicating such. Because of her refusal, in January 2005 officials extended her eighteen-month sentence by another three months.

Lin lives in China.

Though Roya's (not her real name) **prepubescent** body developed like that of any girl her age, her mind remained that of an eight-year-old. The young girl would never develop mentally and emotionally like her peers.

Roya's mother solved the problem of having a mentally delayed child by forcing her handicapped daughter into prostitution when the child was only eight years old. Roya became the easy target for sexual abuse and was repeatedly raped from that time on. The young girl gave birth to her first child when she was just nine years old.

Women in China are only allowed to have two children.

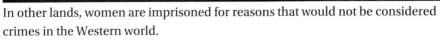

In other lands, women are imprisoned for reasons that would not be considered crimes in the Western world.

Convicted of "prostitution," nine-year-old Roya received a hundred lashes for her crime. Flogging, not imprisonment, is the standard punishment for prostitution in Roya's homeland.

When Roya turned twelve, her mother sold her to a man, who made the adolescent girl his "temporary wife." That man's "permanent wife" became Roya's new pimp and sold the girl to any man who wanted to use her. By the age of fourteen, Roya became pregnant again, and again officials found her guilty of prostitution for which she received a hundred more lashes. When time came for her to deliver, the young girl gave birth to twins.

After her "temporary marriage," ceased, Roya's family sold her one more time—to a fifty-five-year-old married man who sold her to men out of his home. The girl was still in her mid-teens.

In December 2004, officials sentenced nineteen-year-old Roya, who still had a mental age equivalent to that of an eight-year-old, to death for morality crimes. She faces execution because her family forced her into a life of prostitution.

Though detained until her sentence is carried out, Roya has never seen a court-appointed doctor to have her mental ability tested. When officials tried and convicted the teenager, they never considered her background or mental development.

Roya lives in Iran.

Ham and Chu (not their real names) traveled to a neighboring country as representatives of a student organization working toward peace. While there, the two female college students visited universities and tourist sites and met with other students and local officials. When they returned to their homeland, both were arrested and sentenced to serve three years in jail for taking an unauthorized visit to the neighboring country.

Though Amnesty International could not verify the conditions of women's imprisonment at the time of this writing, the human rights organization details what the two might expect.

According to Amnesty International reports, women held in the students' homeland are detained and housed separately from men.

The political conditions in some countries severely limit women's rights.

FAST FACTS FROM THE U.S. BUREAU OF JUSTICE STATISTICS

- In the United States in 1999, state and federal prisons housed an estimated 721,500 parents (men and women) of nearly 1.5 million children under the age of eighteen.
- More than half of the mothers housed in state prisons reported never having had a personal visit with their children since the time of their imprisonments.
- Over 60 percent of incarcerated parents report being housed in facilities located more than a hundred miles from the last place of known residence.
- Almost 200,000 minor children in the United States have a mother who is incarcerated.
- Nearly 60 percent of these children were ten years old or younger.

Generally, female inmates find it difficult to obtain clothing and footwear in appropriate sizes because most prison uniforms are designed for men. Most female prisoners find it next to impossible to obtain sanitary products, undergarments, and other items necessary for personal hygiene. Access to medical treatment is rare.

Women political prisoners, like the two students, are held in solitary confinement, segregated from other prisoners and allowed little or no human contact for the duration of their sentences. One political prisoner held in the same prison where the two students are incarcerated stated on her release that she was kept in solitary confinement for three years

Women all over the world are imprisoned for drug-related crimes.

and not permitted to speak with other inmates. When she was released, she had difficulty talking because her vocal chords had not been used for so long.

These women live in South Korea.

China, Iran, and South Korea are not the only countries known to treat women inmates unjustly. In Pakistan, for example, women prisoners report being slapped, suspended from ceilings, beaten, and having their private body areas violated with objects including police batons and chili peppers (the oils of which cause extreme burning pain).

Even in developed nations, like we've seen in some of the issues faced by women inmates in the United States, female prisoners suffer violations of treatment standards set by international law.

What happens to women when they are arrested, how they are tried, convicted, sentenced, and treated after sentencing varies greatly from nation to nation. One thing UN researchers found all surveyed countries had in common, however, was this: by far, the greatest numbers of perpetrators of crime are men, regardless of race, nationality, culture, or religion. In Western Samoa, for example, a UN study estimates that for every female criminal suspect, officials arrest ninety-one male suspects. Worldwide, the problem of incarcerated men appears to be far more prevalent an issue than that of incarcerated women.

Despite the fact that overall, women make up a small percentage of the total prison populations worldwide, a study commissioned by the Quaker United Nations Office concluded, "women prisoners suffer poor physical and mental health at rates and with a severity far exceeding those of male prisoners or of women in the general population."

Some of this may be explained by the fact that women all over the world are imprisoned for similar offenses to those of their North American counterparts: drugs or drug-related crimes. Part of this may be explained by the trauma imprisoned mothers face when they're separated from their children and families. It may also be due, in part, to the severe overcrowding occurring in the women's prisons today throughout the world.

Though often held in coed facilities, male/female prisoners seldom have contact.

THE INTERNATIONAL COVENANT ON CIVIL AND POLITICAL RIGHTS (ICCPR)

The ICCPR, an international treaty that sets guidelines for the treatment of all civil and political detainees, established the following rights and protections for all people regardless of gender, race, or any other distinction:

1. The right not to be subjected to torture or cruel, inhuman, or degrading treatment or punishment (Article 7).
2. The right of any detained person to be treated with humanity and with respect to the inherent dignity of the human person (Article 10).
3. The right to privacy without arbitrary interference (Article 17).

In most countries, women who commit crime serve time behind bars, but why and how they get there, and what happens to them while in state custody, varies dramatically from country to country depending on each nation's culture and laws. How they are treated also depends on how many women in that country commit crime.

In Mexico, for example, the traditionally low number of female prisoners means that few prisons exist just for them. Of 447 Mexican prisons, only 10 house women alone. In England and Wales, 125 prisons exist for men and only 16 for women. In India, nearly 11,000 jails exist of which only 14 are reserved for women.

Imagine being housed with nearly 600 female prisoners in a building designed for 250, as is the case in one women's prison in Brazil. Think about the lack of bathroom accessibility incarcerated women in Egypt faced when 1,100 women were forced to share facilities designed to hold 500 men. In one prison in Bolivia, four women detainees and 600

REGIONS WITH THE HIGHEST PERCENTAGES OF FEMALE INMATES

(numbers indicate the percentage of the total prison population that is female)

1. Maldive Islands: 26.6 percent
2. Hong Kong (China): 21.6 percent
3. Thailand: 18.4 percent
4. Bolivia: 12.1 percent
5. Qatar: 11.8 percent
6. Paraguay: 11.3 percent
7. Singapore: 11.0 percent
8. Bermuda (United Kingdom): 10.5 percent
9. Aruba (Netherlands): 10.0 percent
10. Macau (China): 9.7 percent
11. Netherlands: 8.8 percent
12. Cayman Islands (United Kingdom): 8.6 percent

Of 174 countries, the United States is tied for thirteenth on the list with 8.4 percent of its prison population being female. Canada is tied for sixty-fourth, with 5.0 percent of inmates being female.

children were made to share a space measuring only 323 square feet (30 meters) square.

Overcrowding of women prisons is a problem not just in North America where tens of thousands of women serve their time, but all over the world.

Treatment of women prisoners has become a global concern. A UN report titled *Global Report on Crime and Justice* concludes simply that "crime is everywhere." Even though various countries define crime differently and even though they treat criminal offenders according to differing laws and guidelines, no country is immune to the problem of crime and what to do with those who commit crimes. And no country has solved the problem of what to do with its female prisoners.

Awareness of the need to deal with women prisoners does not mean prison officials treat women inmates with dignity and respect all over the world. In fact, most women prisoners worldwide face issues that are far greater than those of their incarcerations: second-class status in cultures dominated by men; extreme and severe punishments, like flogging or stoning, imposed on women in lieu of jail time; swift and merciless punishment when convicted with little hope for appeal; little or no voice in justice issues, and lack of adequate representation in the court process.

These issues fall well outside the scope of this book, but women serving time in many other countries (particularly developing nations) face not only the same special issues women inmates face in American prisons (a shortage of adequate mental health care, the need for better medical care, the need for protection from sexual abuse, etc.), but they face gender hurdles imposed by cultural and religious prejudices as well.

Thankfully, though the picture could seem bleak for women behind bars, some recent innovations in programming and treatment of women prisoners seem to be improving the outlook for women in the criminal justice system overall.

CHAPTER 7

HELPING WOMEN INMATES: WHAT WORKS?

"I just signed the checks to get medical care," Margaret explains in *Women in Prison: Inside the Concrete Tomb* as she recounts the details of her arrest and conviction for insufficient funds and intent to defraud. "My husband wouldn't help me and I didn't have any other money. I wasn't getting proper medical care until I came here. There's a lot of things wrong with the hospital here, but at least I'm getting attention.

"Coming here has done me a lot of good. This was the best thing that could have happened to me 'cause now I have the chance to start a new life. People here have helped me. When I first came in here I was scared of my shadow. When I leave here, I'm gonna start a new life to prove to the people here they've helped me."

"When I got this sentence here, the court put me on methadone," says Trinada, convicted of narcotics possessions and intent to sell (as quoted in *Women in Prison: Inside the Concrete Tomb*). "So when I get out with that help, and my own, I should stay drug free.

"A place like this, there's less chance of any type of drugs or alcohol getting into the institution. Here, it's discipline. You learn to control yourself. . . . It's telling me, 'You can do without,' . . . so I guess it's good for me.

"My main fear now is, will I be able to maintain myself without getting involved in any things that are unnecessary? I have a real fear of getting busted and returned. And I don't wanna face no twenty years in the penitentiary. I don't wanna die in no penitentiary. So I'm gonna try. Just try and maintain myself. I know I can make it."

"If I am granted parole I know I can make it outside of prison, because I am a different person now than when I first came here," says Delia in a letter to her parole board, as quoted in *The Farm: Life Inside a Women's Prison*. "My family and friends are very supportive and proud of me.

"I have been working very hard with counselors from addiction services on my low self-esteem and insecurities (that resulted from a tragic childhood!). Most of all we have been focusing on my long history of alcohol, physical, and mental abuse. Today I am focusing on my on-going recovery.

"I have used all resources and support here. I attended and completed behavior studies, recovery and co-dependency groups; attended AA and church (as much as my health would allow me). I plan to do the same when I am released."

Margaret, Trinada, and Delia found help in prison, as do thousands of incarcerated women in North America each year. Despite many of the challenges facing prison officials in charge of women inmates today, many prisons are successfully rehabilitating the women in their charge while addressing their unique needs. Some programs *do* work.

The Eddie Warrior Correctional Center in Oklahoma offers two programs targeting female inmates who have children. One program is called

WOMEN IN PRISON

Women in prison face many challenges.

Children's Play Day and the other is called Parenting. The women must participate in Parenting, a practical parenting skills class, before they can participate in Children's Play Day, a program designed to maintain the bond between an incarcerated mother and her children. The children are transported by volunteers to the prisons where their mothers serve their time for scheduled days of play and recreation.

The newly opened Fraser Valley Institution for Women, which services women under federal jurisdiction in Canada, offers several up-to-date programs designed to meet a female inmate's needs: substance abuse treatment, survivors of sexual abuse and trauma programs, psychiatric care, spiritual services, programs for specific minority populations (including **Aboriginal** inmates), emotional and behavioral management classes, education and job training, premium physical and mental health services (which are offered on site at the facility's Health Care Centre), and programs designed to help inmates transition into the community. Fraser Valley also makes a private family visiting house available to women for scheduling visits with their families. Another house is designated for the Fraser Valley Mother-Child Program, which seeks to help mothers maintain regular contact with their children during their prison terms.

The Canadian Association of Elizabeth Fry Societies offers programs and support for women involved in Canada's criminal justice system all over the country. The Societies, as they are known in Canada, provide counseling, support, education, training, and other programs for women and their children throughout the inmates' prison experiences. For released prisoners, the Societies fund **halfway houses**, shelters, job-hunting services, job-training workshops, telephone crisis lines, and support groups. In British Columbia, Elizabeth Fry Societies offer the Sexual Assault Support Healing and Advocacy Program for women who survived past abuse or recent assault.

The Grant House in Toronto, Ontario, fills a different need. Designed to be a long-term residential facility, the house takes in up to ten former inmates with histories of substance abuse, and encourages them to maintain their sobriety after release from prison. Using community resources and programs including Alcoholics Anonymous, Narcotics

WOMEN IN PRISON

ORGANIZATIONS ADVOCATING FOR WOMEN PRISONERS AROUND THE WORLD

Amnesty International
Human Rights Watch
International Committee of the Red Cross
Stop Prisoner Rape
Elizabeth Fry Societies (Canada)
Howard League for Penal Reform (Canada)
American Civil Liberties Union (United States)
Women in Prison (United Kingdom)
218.org (United Kingdom)

Anonymous, and Cocaine Anonymous, residents find the help they need to successfully overcome their addictions.

A program in Portland, Oregon, focuses on women convicted of prostitution. Called the Council on Prostitution Alternatives, this program offers women a four-stage program that equips them to leave the life that landed them in jail in the first place. The program includes counseling, practical support (food, clothing, financial help), education, job training, life skills classes, parenting programs, health education classes, support groups, and emergency services.

These few programs represent hundreds of new initiatives committed to helping women transition from prison to public life taking place across North America today. While the United States in particular has much to do to improve its handling of women in prison, each new program and initiative takes us closer to ensuring justice for all.

GLOSSARY

Aboriginal: A member of any of the peoples who inhabited Canada before the arrival of European settlers.

advocate: Someone who supports or speaks in favor of something.

asylum: Protection from arrest and extradition.

bipolar disorder: A psychiatric disorder characterized by mood swings ranging between extreme highs and extreme lows.

borderline personality disorder: A psychological condition characterized by emotional instability and marked by self-destructive, manipulative, and erratic behavior.

chronic depression: A psychiatric disorder extending over a long period or frequently recurring, characterized by persistent feelings of hopelessness, poor concentration, lack of energy, and inability to sleep.

exploitation: The unfair treatment or use of somebody or someone for personal gain.

halfway houses: Residences for those who have been released from an institution (such as a mental hospital or prison), designed to help individuals readjust to "life on the outside."

paranoid: A psychiatric disorder characterized by obsessive anxiety about something or unreasonable suspicion about other people and their thoughts or motives.

parole: The early release of a prisoner with specified requirements, such as the need to report to authorities for a specified period.

pimped: Sold as prostitutes.

prepubescent: The stage of life just before puberty.

protocols: Detailed rules and plans.

redress: Compensation for a loss.

retribution: Punishment.

schizoid personality: A condition characterized by, tending toward, or suggestive of schizophrenia.

WOMEN IN PRISON

schizophrenia: A psychotic disorder characterized by a loss of contact with the environment, a noticeable deterioration in the level of functioning on an everyday basis, and disordered feelings, thoughts, perceptions, and behaviors.

stigma: Mark of shame or discredit.

victimization: The action of making someone a victim.

watchdog: Having to do with guarding against dishonest or undesirable practices.

FURTHER READING

Bode, Janet, and Stan Mack. *Hard Time: A Real Life Look at Juvenile Crime and Violence*. New York: Delacorte Press, 1996.

Butler, Anne M. *Gendered Justice in the American West: Women Prisoners in Men's Penitentiaries*. Chicago: University of Illinois Press, 2000.

Chevigny, Bell Gale, ed. *Doing Time: 25 Years of Prison Writings*. New York: Arcade Publishing, 1999.

Gordon, Robert Ellis, and Inmates of the Washington Corrections System. *The Funhouse Mirror: Reflections on Prison*. Pullman: Washington State University Press, 2000.

Grapes, Bryan J. *Prisons*. San Diego, Calif.: Greenhaven Press, 2000.

Herman, Peter G., ed. *The American Prison System*. Bronx, N.Y.: The H. W. Wilson Company, 2001.

Hjelmeland, Andy. *Inside the Big House*. Minneapolis, Minn.: Lerner, 1996.

Lamb, Wally, and the Women of York Correctional Institution. *Couldn't Keep It to Myself: Testimonies from Our Imprisoned Sisters*. New York: HarperCollins, 2003.

Newton, Michael. *Bad Girls Do It! An Encyclopedia of Female Murderers*. Port Townsend, Wash.: Loompanics Unlimited, 1993.

Rierden, Andi. *The Farm: Life Inside a Women's Prison*. Amherst: University of Massachusetts Press, 1997.

Stewart, Gail B. *Teens in Prison*. San Diego, Calif.: Lucent Books, 1997.

Williams, Stanley "Tookie." *Life in Prison*. San Francisco, Calif.: Sea Star Books, 1998.

WOMEN IN PRISON

FOR MORE INFORMATION

American Civil Liberties Union (ACLU)
www.aclu.org

American Corrections Association
www.corrections.com

Canadian Families and Corrections Network
www3.sympatico.ca/cfcn

Coalition for Juvenile Justice (CJJ)
www.juvjustice.org

Federal Bureau of Prisons (BOP)
www.bop.gov

Human Rights Watch
www.hrw.org

Justice for Girls
www.justiceforgirls.org

Juvenile Information Network
www.juvenilenet.org

National Institute of Corrections (NIC)
nicic.org

National Criminal Justice Reference Service (NCJRS)
www.ncjrs.org

Office of Juvenile Justice and Delinquency Prevention (OJJDP)
ojjdp.ncjrs.org

Prisoners HIV/AIDS Support Action Network (PASAN)
www.pasan.org

The Other Side of the Wall
www.prisonwall.org

The Prison Policy Initiative
www.prisonsucks.com

U.S. Department of Justice (USDOJ)
www.usdoj.gov

USDOJ's Bureau of Justice Assistance (BJA)
www.ojp.usdoj.gov/BJA

USDOJ's Bureau of Justice Statistics
www.ojp.usdoj.gov/bjs/welcome.html

Publisher's note:
The Web sites listed on these pages were active at the time of publication. The publisher is not responsible for Web sites that have changed their addresses or discontinued operation since the date of publication. The publisher will review and update the Web-site list upon each reprint.

BIBLIOGRAPHY

Gonnerman, Jennifer. *Life on the Outside: The Prison Odyssey of Elaine Bartlett.* New York: Picador USA, 2005.

Harris, M. K. "Women's Imprisonment in the United States: A Historical Analysis." *Corrections Today*, December 1, 1998.

Sharp, Susan F., and Roslyn Muraskin. *The Incarcerated Woman: Rehabilitative Programming in Woman's Prisons.* Upper Saddle River, N.J.: Pearson Education, 2003.

"Women in Prison." http://www.prisonactivist.org/women/women-in-prison.html.

"Women's Human Rights." Amnesty International USA. http://www.amnestyusa.org/women/womeninprison.html.

Women's Prison Association. http://www.wpaonline.org.

INDEX

WOMEN IN PRISON

PICTURE CREDITS

Benjamin Stewart: pp. 92, 99
Brand X: pp. 32, 33, 51, 52, 55, 74
Corbis: p. 34
iStock: p. 73
 Andrei Orlov: p. 67
 Anita Patterson: p. 12
 Christina Fumi: p. 68
 Dane Wirtzfield: p. 57
 Dirk Diesel: pp. 22, 29
 Heidi Kristensen: p. 60
 Jennifer Steele: p. 44
 Jonathan Ling: p. 36
 Justin Horrocks: p. 18
 Karen Grotzinger: p. 11
 Mark Evans: p. 69
 Martin Youssef: p. 88
 Roberto Adrian: p. 46
 Rosina N. Burge: p. 86
 Suzanne Tucker: p. 58
 Thomas Pullicino: p. 10
Jupiter Images: pp. 30, 42, 70, 76, 78, 79, 80, 85, 90
Photodisc: p. 16

To the best knowledge of the publisher, all other images are in the public domain. If any image has been inadvertently uncredited, please notify Harding House Publishing Service, Vestal, New York 13850, so that rectification can be made for future printings.

Chapter opening art was taken from a painting titled *Blue Door 1* by Raymond Gray.

Raymond Gray has been incarcerated since 1973. Mr. Gray has learned from life, and hard times, and even from love. His artwork reflects all of these.

BIOGRAPHIES

AUTHOR

Joan Esherick is the author of twenty nonfiction books and dozens of articles in national and international publications on a variety of subjects. She lives in Pennsylvania with her husband of twenty-three years and their three nearly grown children.

SERIES CONSULTANT

Dr. Larry E. Sullivan is Associate Dean and Chief Librarian at the John Jay College of Criminal Justice and Professor of Criminal Justice in the doctoral program at the Graduate School and University Center of the City University of New York. He first became involved in the criminal justice system when he worked at the Maryland Penitentiary in Baltimore in the late 1970s. That experience prompted him to write the book *The Prison Reform Movement: Forlorn Hope* (1990; revised edition 2002). His most recent publication is the three-volume *Encyclopedia of Law Enforcement* (2005). He has served on a number of editorial boards, including the *Encyclopedia of Crime and Punishment,* and *Handbook of Transnational Crime and Justice.* At John Jay College, in addition to directing the largest and best criminal justice library in the world, he teaches graduate and doctoral level courses in criminology and corrections. John Jay is the only liberal arts college with a criminal justice focus in the United States. Internationally recognized as a leader in criminal justice education and research, John Jay is also a major training facility for local, state, and federal law enforcement personnel.